# My Canada
# ONTARIO

By Sheila Yazdani

## TABLE OF CONTENTS

Ontario . . . . . . . . . . . . . . . . . . . . . . . . 3

Glossary . . . . . . . . . . . . . . . . . . . . . . 22

Index . . . . . . . . . . . . . . . . . . . . . . . . 24

A Crabtree Seedlings Book

Crabtree Publishing
crabtreebooks.com

# School-to-Home Support for Caregivers and Teachers

This book helps children grow by letting them practice reading. Here are a few guiding questions to help the reader build his or her comprehension skills. Possible answers appear in red.

## Before Reading:

- What do I know about Ontario?
    - *I know that Ontario is a province.*
    - *I know that Ontario has many lakes.*

- What do I want to learn about Ontario?
    - *I want to learn which famous people were born in Ontario.*
    - *I want to learn what the provincial flag looks like.*

## During Reading:

- What have I learned so far?
    - *I have learned that Toronto is the capital of Ontario.*
    - *I have learned that more than 2,867 metric tons (3,160 tons) of water go over Niagara Falls every second.*

- I wonder why…
    - *I wonder why the provincial flower is the white trillium.*
    - *I wonder why Ontario grows so many grapes.*

## After Reading:

- What did I learn about Ontario?
    - *I have learned that the CN Tower is 553 meters (1,814 feet) tall.*
    - *I have learned that the provincial bird is the common loon.*

- Read the book again and look for the glossary words.
    - *I see the word **capital** on page 6, and the word **shield** on page 12. The other glossary words are found on pages 22 and 23.*

I live in St. Catharines. It is known as "The Garden City."

My city has the Royal Canadian Henley **Regatta** every August.

Ontario is a **province** in central Canada. The **capital** is Toronto.

Fun Fact: Toronto is the largest city in Ontario.

The provincial bird is the common loon.

Fun Fact: Ontario grows more than 77,000 metric tons (85,000 tons) of grapes a year.

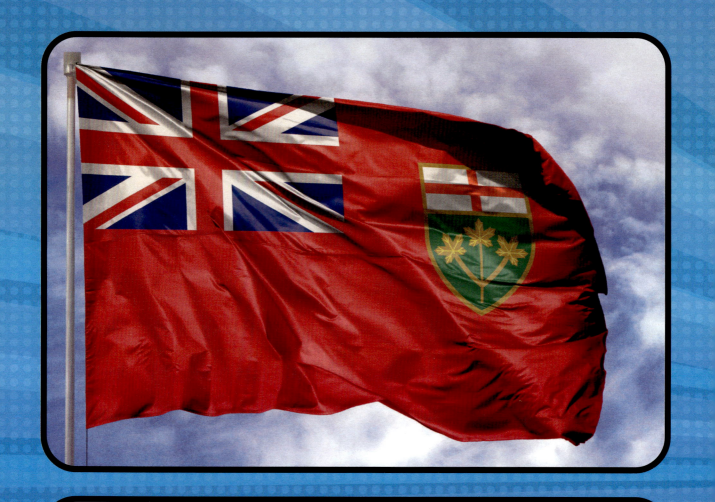

My provincial flag is red.
It has a **Union Jack** and a **shield** on it.

My family likes to watch the Toronto Blue Jays play baseball.

I can visit the **Parliament** Buildings in Ottawa.

My family goes canoeing on Lake Huron.

Actor Ryan Gosling was born in Ontario. Alex Trebek, former host of the TV game show *Jeopardy!*, was also born in Ontario.

Fun Fact: Astronaut Chris Hadfield, the first Canadian to walk in space, was born in Sarnia, Ontario.

My family likes to go for boat rides around the Thousand Islands.

# Glossary

**capital** (CAP-ih-tuhl): The city or town where the government of a country, state, or province is located

**parliament** (PAR-luh-muhnt): The group of people who make the laws for a country

**province** (PROV-ins): One of the large areas that some countries, such as Canada, are divided into

**regatta** (ri-GAH-tuh): A boat race

**shield** (sheeld): A picture that is shaped like a soldier's shield

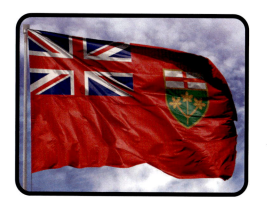

**Union Jack** (YOON-yuhn jak): The flag of the United Kingdom

# Index

canoeing 17
common loon 8
Gosling, Ryan 18
grapes 10, 11
Niagara Falls 15
Toronto 6, 7

# About the Author

Sheila Yazdani lives in Ontario near Niagara Falls with her dog Daisy. She likes to travel across Canada to learn about its history, people, and landscape. She loves to cook new dishes she learns about. Her favorite treat is Nanaimo bars.

Written by: Sheila Yazdani
Designed and Illustrated by: Bobbie Houser
Series Development: James Earley
Proofreader: Melissa Boyce
Educational Consultant: Marie Lemke M.Ed.

Photographs:
Alamy: James Hackland: p. 4; Thomas Kitchin & Victoria Hurst: p. 5, 23; Max Simson: 14-15; NASA Archive: p. 19
Newscom: Julian Avram/Icon Sportswire DFW: p. 13
Shutterstock: Aqnus Febriyant: cover; JFunk: p. 3; Media Guru: p. 6, 22; Stephane Legrand: p. 7; Jim Cumming: p. 8; Craig Sterken: p. 9; Gilberto Mesquita: p. 10-11; nutt: p. 11; Millenius: p. 12, 23; Jam Norasett: p. 15; Natalia Pushchina: p. 16, 22; LesPalenik: p. 17; DFree: p. 18 left; Kathy Hutchins: p. 18 right; LesPalenik: p. 20; Diego Grandi: p. 21

# Crabtree Publishing

crabtreebooks.com    800-387-7650
Copyright © 2025 Crabtree Publishing
All rights reserved. No part of this publication may be reproduced, stored in a retrieval system or be transmitted in any form or by any means, electronic, mechanical, photocopying, recording, or otherwise, without the prior written permission of Crabtree Publishing. In Canada: We acknowledge the financial support of the Government of Canada through the Canada Book Fund for our publishing activities.
Printed in Canada/012024/CP20231127

Published in Canada
Crabtree Publishing
616 Welland Avenue
St. Catharines, Ontario
L2M 5V6

Published in the United States
Crabtree Publishing
347 Fifth Avenue
Suite 1402-145
New York, New York, 10016

**Library and Archives Canada Cataloguing in Publication**
Available at Library and Archives Canada

**Library of Congress Cataloging-in-Publication Data**
Available at the Library of Congress

Hardcover: 978-1-0398-3858-1
Paperback: 978-1-0398-3943-4
Ebook (pdf): 978-1-0398-4024-9
Epub: 978-1-0398-4096-6